WALKING IN TWO WORLDS

What people say about Margaret Hurdman

"The most incredible person that I have ever had the pleasure to meet. Please believe me, Margaret is the real deal. From partial sceptic to true believer, thank you Margaret."

Steven 12/07/11

"I was blessed with the opportunity to meet Margaret Hurdman in the UK in March 2007. Margaret's gifts of connecting with the Spirit World are unlike anything I have ever or since experienced. The words communicated from Spirit through Margaret were loving, transformative and validating, and gave me hope and the courage to make the life changes I knew I had to make. Margaret Hurdman truly is a blessed gift unto all of creation."

Naomi – Canada 24/04/2011

"I was lucky enough to be able to attend the Event in Guernsey last August. It was an amazing time for me as I went with an open but cynical mind and you did not disappoint. We spoke to you after the event in the lobby and my grandmother came through to you. You'll be pleased to hear that some of what she said has helped."

Sarah – Guernsey 24/04/2011

"I attended in Newtown Abbey October 2008 and the evening was brilliant. You are truly an inspiration to others. The detail you went in to with people was excellent. The difference with you from other Mediums is that you care about the person. Well done."

Joanne – County Antrim

"I first met Margaret in February this year, a week before I was about to undergo major surgery. I cannot adequately describe the comfort, strength and healing she gave me at a very vulnerable time in my life. Since that first meeting we have become friends."

Simon

Walking in two worlds

Margaret Hurdman

Published by **Librario Publishing Ltd**
ISBN 978-1-906775-22-3

Copies can be ordered:
> from retail
> via the internet at: www.librario.com
> or from:
  Brough House
  Kinloss
  Moray IV36 2UA
  Scotland

Typefaces: ITC Garamond (text), Quadraat (cover)
Design and layout: Omnis Partners, Cumbernauld
Printed and bound in Great Britain

Contents

The real me

I can honestly say that I have met so many interesting people in my life. I appear to be full of confidence, please do not let yourself be fooled, I am confident in the work I do yet as a person I doubt myself all the time. I frequently ask of Spirit, "Why did I fall for that? Why did I allow myself to be hurt by people sometimes using and abusing my trust repeatedly?" I am reminded it's my fault for allowing these happenings and of course we have the greatest gift of all, Free Will.

So I have to say to myself, "Margaret, don't blame anyone, only you are to blame for your actions". We are responsible for our actions and have no right to moan and blame others. I am very lucky in the way that I have a very special husband who, in these later days of my work, travels with me; this is a great comfort for who knows me better than he does? Nobody, I can become ratty when I have a lot on my mind and I do take people's problems on board. I shouldn't but I do and that's who I am. We have been married now fifty-three years. He deserves a medal; I am not an easy person to live with and I would be lost without him. One has to work at marriage, I didn't realise at one time that this in itself is a full time job. I think at long last I now know how not to burn his toast.

Our three sons are very protective and I consider myself lucky that I have three special daughters, my daughters-in-law so we have been doubly blessed. People ask of me, "Do your sons have your gift?" I know they are aware and have seen Spirit yet it is my grandchildren who share the insight. I always knew Sarah sensed and now I find that my eldest grand-daughter, Nicola is more and more aware. It is their choice if they wish to enlarge on the knowledge and I will help them if they choose to do so. I do not pretend that this work is all sweetness; it isn't, there are times when it would be easier to scrub floors to earn one's bread. Even though this way of life can be lucrative it certainly is not the easiest.

I find myself very bound up with charities and I hope I can continue to do so. I must destroy the myth that food appears on a plate and money appears in one's handbag as if by magic. It certainly absent in mine and while a lot of my work is given freely, I still try to earn a salary since it is costly to travel and stay in hotels. Theatres also have their expenses, and when you see me on stage I dress up because I represent Spirit. But I confess I am a keen Oxfam and charity shop investor for my bits and pieces. The real me is the scruffy woman, no make up and sloppy jumper, probably with flour over her skirt and disgustingly old slippers who answers the door to the postman, – that's Margaret the person.

So my friend, if you think the World of the Medium is a glamorous one, forget that notion, I assure you it is not. Often a phone rings when you are just going to bed, someone in trouble or sickness. To some you are a voice of comfort, to others you are there to unburden upon. Most people feel a trouble shared is a troubled halved and perhaps I should say no, yet I can't. It is my nature and I would like to think that there will be someone at the end of a telephone line for my loved ones if needed.

If I have painted a glum outlook to you I am sorry. The truth is I would not change what I do, and hope that I have been a little bit of help to someone on their path of life.

One thing I must point out is that sometimes I wish I could have for myself what is given to me for others. I understand this, what I have with Spirit is not for me. Sometimes I am made aware of problems with my family, yet my gift, if you call it that, is for others. Someone asked me for the winning lottery numbers; how little they know, that is not my purpose of life.

While money is not everything it certainly helps to smooth the way. Perhaps the lack of it is why my path has always been rocky.

Walking in two worlds

Looking back I have always wondered why I have been given the insight into the Spirit World.

I am an ordinary person with ordinary feelings, in every way a human being of the usual sort. Why does Spirit wish to work with me? My life changed for me when I visited the Spirit World, and was pronounced dead. I was in my thirties during what was then a very major operation, open heart surgery, and I believe I am the longest surviving patient. This has been the base of my finding out the truth, the reason we live and the reason we die, no not die but move onto a better understanding of spheres and existence of the human soul.

I have very little education regarding academic things; my education is life and the ups and downs of living. I know I still have tasks to do and I hope my health will see me through to do what is expected of me. God only knows.

I remember asking many questions in the beginning of my awareness of Spirit. Why me? I received the answer from Spirit, my special Friend and Guide Abe;

> *"Because you will speak from the heart, and only if you suffer yourself can you understand the suffering of others."*

How very true this was, I now understand fully. Life is a learning time yet how much learning can one do and how much acceptance can we accept?

As a Medium there are times when I have doubted my sanity. I have questioned myself, did I see that or is it an optical illusion? Did I really hear that? One must question, all the time.

If we do not we become complacent, perhaps over egotistical. I believe one of the major tests to me happened when I was diagnosed with kidney cancer. Again the doubting Thomas came through, why me?

The night before my admission to hospital seemed endless. I tossed and turned, the room filled with an amazing light, clearly I saw my children discussing me, they were talking about me and the personal things that I have. I heard them in my mind saying, "Don't give that away. Mom loved that jacket". Then I visualised my husband talking to them about my life and my wishes. I felt like shouting, "Hi you lot, I am here, still around". Next moment I was back in the now, and I said to Abe how cruel that was to which he replied;

"You are blessed so are your family, they know there is no end to loving, make sure you tell others."

I wasn't impressed - would you be? As you can see I survived the operation and am still carrying on with the work I love, giving hope and comfort when needed.

First things first, let me explain how the world of awareness works: the communicator is the Spirit wishing to talk to the recipient, who is the sitter, 'the client'.

The doorkeeper is the helper who stands at all my sittings and sifts the energy, in other words guards and protects against negative thoughts and disturbing energy. I always welcome the assistance of this special energy. If you do not feel comfortable within the area you are going to work, do not work. Trust in your intuition.

Personally, I like to play a little light music and sit and enjoy my peace before a client arrives. Always close down and make sure that the energy that you have worked with is clear at the end of a sitting. I visualize a blanket of white washing the room; this then is ready for another time.

What makes a medium?

There are so many ways of working with Spirit, there are many roles to fill and many ways to serve. I found the hardest lesson was not to be impatient, to take one step at a time and take on board what your own gut feelings tell you.

There are many good books on development and there are many energies that surround me and ask to let me see with a clear honest mind. I make sure I am sitting on a backed chair, my feet firmly on the ground and I imagine my energy coming from my feet up through my body to the top of my head and flowing over and forming a lovely cloak of white.

Never cross your arms in front of your Solar Plexus, be comfy, warm and at ease. There is nothing to fear, then ask your guide and helpers to work with you.

I also have my own little prayer I use:

'I am a child of God and I will accept nothing that is not of God.'

The closing down is again up to you as an individual, this is my way:

I imagine a light, I unclip and place in God's care. I start at the top of my head and imagine closing over the crown Chakra, the top of the head. I then drain the energy to the third eye in the middle of the forehead, try to picture a dustbin lid closing, and buff. Drain the energy again to the throat Chakra; close the lid over, buff. Then the middle of the chest, then down to the heart carrying on to the belly button, the Solar Plexus, then to Base Chakra, then feet and then to the ground.

I always try and clear all thoughts that have been around me. In all ways closing the energy, draining all to the earth and being fully grounded. Some people use different ways. I have colleagues who imagine washing their bodies and all around them; someone else I know puts himself in a glass jar. As long as it does the job and you are free of lingering thoughts and energy that's all that matters.

These are the guidelines I would always follow:

Try to be aware and honest. Sometimes we do not always say exactly what we feel or see, do not embroider with our own thoughts. Do not guess, if you are not sure what spirit says always ask for more proof, more information. We must always be honest. Remember if the Spirit is a bossy person or self centred, often they will apologize especially if they know they need to change their outlook. However their personality very often stays the same.

I stress strongly that Spirit will not hurt you. Should you find yourself not happy with the communicator or the information, then challenge. If I find myself challenging I always ask "Are you of the light?" "Is that what you really mean?" You must make sure there is no dark energy. However I find the living will hurt you more often than not if you allow them.

Be aware of your senses. What do you smell? What do you feel? You may find your self aware of certain senses, for example, the scent of a particular perfume or the smell of pipe tobacco, or maybe even an urge to scratch or rub a certain part of your body – this would have been a habit of the communicator. We need to look to look out for these clues so we can determine who the communicator is.

Be aware of being shown symbols, these can often be so ordinary but often convey a different meaning. I have had Spirit showing me some fish and chips and since Spirit doesn't lie, this gentleman had owned a fish and chip shop.

A medium's dream is to discover names and addresses but this rarely happens. Names are not important to me, it is the energy that speaks to me, the feelings and memories of Spirit that are important when I work.

There is no end to experiences or happenings. It is an ever growing circle, and these are a few of my travelling happenings.

Lingering energy

Many things have happened to me since I wrote my last book. Whilst I remember all the incidents there's one that stands out in my mind, which is the area of trouble or Spirits that are trapped and need help. During one of my demonstrations, I was drawn to a lady in the audience. My Guide, Abe, said that her home was badly troubled, as were a lot of the houses on the estate. I asked her to speak with me after the show because what I was seeing was that the disturbed energy around her estate was causing trouble for her family and I knew I could help her with the help of my Spirit guides. We went to the house the next day and immediately I was drawn to a field opposite where building work was taking place; apparently as the land diggers were working they had found some underground tunnels which the IRA had dug in the past. Some men had been trapped in them and their Spirits were confused. So with my helpers we spoke and helped the soldiers to move on. The young lady whose house we were in was concerned that it would stop the loving energy of her mother around her, she was happy knowing it would not do this. Sometimes past vibrations can linger especially if there is sadness.

Another side of this work is dealing with the energy that lingers to objects and land. If a Spirit was particularly fond of a certain object e.g. a chair, they can often be felt around that chair and are reluctant to move on, materialistic thoughts do remain and can hold Spirits back.

Another example I can give is that of a very dear friend who gave me her electric Christmas tree. I guarantee that every Christmas when that tree is put up my old friend is very obvious, she loved it as I do and I have heard her say, "Isn't it lovely my dear." My reply is, "Yes, I am looking after it". Then I smelt her familiar smell of olbas oil, which she used very liberally. That was fourteen years ago and she still watches over her tree; we call it 'May's tree'.

There is a great difference between rescue work and clearance. Sometimes, the energy of the grounds holds past memories which can linger. For instance, the ground of a battlefield which can be so uneasy and often cries, notices and vibrations can be felt of the past. In another example, certain properties can be sad. Often negative energy needs to be lifted, and this is an unusual aspect of spiritual work. I truly feel in these troubled times that ground clearance work is becoming more and more needed and the time will come when we will need more enlightenment and healing of vibrations and energy patterns. There is much to learn on this very important side of this work.

We speak of Rescue work when someone finds it difficult to leave this earthly existence, perhaps because they feel there were things left undone or they are not sure what to expect and are a little bit lost, not being able to move on. This is where we can help. I talk to the energy explaining that they have moved physically to a different life and time and that I will try to help them, assuring them they are not of my world. Theirs is the world of Heaven and it is a place of happiness. Again I repeat this is not their time anymore as the Spirit World awaits them. Then I send my thoughts and prayers to the higher realms and ask them to come and help this earthly Spirit to move to join them into the life beyond. I always say to the energy that lingers, look upwards to the light, there is no reason not to move forward, forward to higher realms. They will not be lonely or lost ever again, their loved ones are waiting for them. Then I ask the Spirit of the earth-bound one to listen as their loved ones come for them, I visualise a spiral of light like a vortex which is light and love. Then I encourage the earth-bound energy to step into the light. Very often you feel that wonderful feeling of love build up and collect the lost one. I can feel a change in the atmosphere and many times I have received a thank you from them as their new life is such joy.

One time that stands out in my memory is of an old lady who had died as a result of the cruelty of the concentration camps. Because of the state of her dying and her absolute fear she could not adjust and was wandering around. Poor lost soul, she came to me during meditation, and I felt her despair. She was seeking her sons and one daughter. Needless to say they also perished in Auschwitz concentration camp. I felt her despair being a mother myself and understood how she felt; she was always seeking them. Lost in my meditation state she told me their names: David and Peter, they were twins, and her daughter who was the eldest, was called Rachael. She kept crying, "Where are my little ones? Why are they hiding?" Then into my conscious mind I heard Abe, my Guide say:

"Show her the way; her family is waiting for her, she needs help, help her."

I temporarily came back into my own World of understanding and I knew that this was my next task. I had a cup of tea and a sandwich; I can not work on an empty tummy. Some mediums prefer to, not me and always after working I am starving hungry, That's an exaggeration, what I mean is I am very hungry, it's as though my energy has been gobbled up.

I then started to try and help the lady who had come into my mediation. I asked my helpers and angels to be with me, then as usual I sat with my feet very firmly upon the ground, my back as straight as could be. Breathing deeply, I asked for the protection of love and then I said the Lord's Prayer. I was ready and soon the vibrations and the energy around me started to change. The Lady I had visualised in my meditation state materialised. I spoke to her as I would to a living person explaining that her dearly loved family and friends were waiting for her in Heaven. She kept saying "I am looking to see where they are". Again I replied, "They are coming for you" Be at Peace you are not of this World you will soon see them, "they are coming," she sighed, "please".

I heard the gentle chatter of children and heard them say, "Come mama, it has been a long time". Again I visualised and felt a spiral of light descending. I asked the old lady, "Step into that light my dear, all is well your family have been looking for you, they have now found you and you have found them. All is well go, with God". I felt and saw them all rising together into the loving light of God. Just as they were disappearing from sight I heard them call to me, "Shalom, friend". I must admit I felt the joy around me at their reunion.

Even though the children would have been grown up by Earth standards they appeared to her as children, which is what they would be in her heart and memories. This is the type of work that is called Rescue, I call it Reunion.

There is also the more negative side of energy when a destructive energy lingers. Not everyone becomes an enlightened being when dying. 'Old habits die hard', my mother used to say. I strongly believe in the power of prayer and the seeking of the higher levels of wisdom. Some time ago I was asked to help to clear a very depressed energy around a young man. By his own negative thoughts he was bringing in energy of a lower level. The young man concerned was on drugs and booze, in fact very much a disruptive force himself. He said that at night he was not sleeping as he was frightened to close his eyes at what he was seeing,. which was a demonic energy. We spoke together at length and I was very much aware of protecting my own energy and asked for the protective energy of the light workers of Heaven. It seemed as though he had been dealing with forces not of God and was paying the price; he constantly used the 'Ouija Board'.

Part of me said not likely. The other side said in my thoughts, what goes around comes around. Yet I knew I could not walk away, as much as I would have liked to. To start with I had to clear the attachment that was with the young man, it was evil, it was an energy that had attached itself to his aura which accounted for his constant depression, aggressive ways and tiredness. That was not normal for anyone. The young man seemed to be in a living hell, and twice he had tried to take his own life. I asked my special friend Abe, my Guide, to help me. I could see the demonic side to him, the side that was giving him such bad energy and firmly said to the young man that if he touched the 'Ouija Board' again I would wash my hands of him. He said he had learnt his lesson, I prayed he had.

I then challenged the energy, after much confrontation and harsh words; the energy left him and was delegated to disperse and never return.

Then came the healing, that is to heal the aura, which was jagged and torn. The aura is the outer spiritual body; it has to be cleansed and repaired with love, light and understanding, by visualising pure white energy going through all layers, in fact a good washing mentally. In describing it to people I ask them to imagine standing in the shower with water cleansing their aura layer by layer. I use 7 layers and cleanse one after the other; I ask the healing powers of God to heal the tears and the damage done. I ask my friends the healers especially my special friend and co-worker Jim to work with me. I am lucky to have a friend of Earth plane who is the most remarkable man, who has the perception and knowledge of this work, whom I rely on at all times. A very much alive man, it is a privilege to be called his friend as he is mine.

It took the young man a long time to build up his good energy levels again. He knows for certain I will never go back on my word that, should he use the 'Ouija Board' again I do not want to know. The answer is with him and he must use his own free will to remain clear.

I am also reminded that some people are so deluded in their minds that they believe that they hear voices and are told to do certain things. This is not a spiritual thing, it is a mental problem and must not be confused, and this illness is called schizophrenia.

This can be related to drugs and brain patterns that are not right.

This is just a small insight into this side of my work and I stress that I myself need the protection of God and the help of my valued friend the Healer, Jim.

The craw

I spoke to a friend who asked for help, it was relating to a property, a very strange place where so many energies were confused. I then spoke to the very nice couple concerned, who were having problems with their centre. The centre was a garden centre and a collector's haven in many ways. Yet everything seemed to be going wrong even though they themselves had a good solid gift for healing. A really kind couple who had hopes of their business developing along the spiritual path.

The past energy was very strong, no wonder the history went back a long way, back far beyond recent troubled events like many places in Ireland. The Viking energy was there, but much of the energy was from the troubled times of the IRA. The field adjoining the house had been an encampment for English soldiers. At the side of the field was what had been a hospital and sadly a mortuary.

I asked my colleague to tune in; he is a remarkable man with a rare gift for clearing troubled ground. He was originally trained by a very gifted Clergyman and I must say in all fairness if I am going into troubled areas I do ask Jim to scan for me which he can do remotely. He has been such a support to me in all these ways. Jim and I worked together on this property, and I knew I could not have had a more gifted man to work with. His healing gift is well known. He also knows if a person has a negative energy with them or if their aura has been disturbed. Many times Jim has done wonders for me no matter how much a spiritual person protects, often a darker energy will try to get in. I say to anyone on this pathway never be too proud to ask for help, people of like mind e.g. the healer understands, so do other mediums with experience of this type of trouble.

I find the work of clearances on the whole very hard and very draining of energy. However I found this house not as hard or tiring as at first expected, this was due to the work done previously by my good friend Jim whom I am very fortunate to have helping me with my work. The house was full of old energies this I could feel because it was in Lay lines – a residue of water that lingers and can often affect thoughts, words and dead energy. In one room which I found to be icy cold sat an old Spirit man. He was content to be there and was at home. I felt him to be a worker of the land, he was very old and had weather-beaten skin with an old cap and his jacket was threadbare. The owners were happy for him to stay and I could hear him coughing as we walked away.

When I moved outside, I found that there was an old burial site to the far side of the property. I managed to settle that with Jim's help then proceeded to the outer field, where two soldiers were leaning on a stile. I could see tents behind them; in fact it was an army camp. I could see their bewildered expressions. Their uniforms were coarse, rough and they must have been very itchy. They were old looking and reminded me of the WW1 uniforms. One wore a peeked cap and the other had the stump of a leg – he said he had died in the field hospital. The other younger soldier said he wanted to go home to his mom, but was sad and scared of leaving his friend whom he called Archie.

I explained that they didn't belong there any more and asked Spirit to fetch them. I asked the younger man to call to his mother as she was waiting for him and his friend would also go to his loved ones. A shaft of light then hit the ground and surrounded both soldiers and the area seemed to lighten up, even the hedges looked greener. They were at peace and the birds were singing. The proving point was that the atmosphere had also lifted. I then channelled with the owners and found that the Spirit energy were very keen for their place to be a centre of healing and that was what Spirit was trying to get through to them.

Jim's healing energy is first class and I know what he has as a gift he uses well and brings so much peace to life, he gives comfort and protection. He is a good friend of mine and I am ever thankful for the help and support he gives me in my work and as a friend.

An American experience

An insight into my time in the land of the Cherokee Indians.

Some time ago I was working in the area of the Cherokee reservations. The occurrences that were my privilege to experience would be so hard to explain. I could only recount them to someone who has an open mind.

My friend owns a very special place, called Mountain Thyme in the Appalachian Mountains, which are an estimated 500 million years old, where real history is and true knowledge takes over myth. It is about the old energy, Native American way. She has students and others who apply to come on her courses to study the ancient ways of the Native American Indians, keen to learn the old spiritual ways. She teaches, she counsels and sets them on the path to awareness. This place is unique where at times it is as though one is in a time warp, where modern man has not set foot, a place to nurture mind, body and spirit. The ways of the mountains are so majestic; they leave you with a deepest respect for Mother-Earth. The animals and the love of nature are in abundance, so time allows you to heal and the energy rejuvenates. I class my visit there as the most amazing time in my life yet.

I first met Hannah at the School of Medium-ship, Stanstead College. It was again a strange time. I felt a strong bond with her yet could not see where it was leading. When I was asked to go to her place I was a little bit in awe of her, she had immense knowledge where I felt myself a very small ordinary person much older and the worse for wear, health-wise. Why me?

Well I went; I couldn't believe the ordinary old stick in the mud Margaret would be flying on my own at a very vulnerable time in World happenings to the Black Mountains, North Carolina, USA.. I scraped the money together and away I went; that is when

Hannah and I started a different type of friendship. She understands and teaches the old ways of sweat loges and sacred rituals so much part of the Native American ways of life. To her every animal is part of a plan and every type of nature is a way of life. It seems strange when I was there I went through a turbulence in my emotions. I put that down to the higher energies that were working with us. The mountains there are some of the most ancient and spectacular places in the world.. Nature is abundant, stepped in history and traditions. These old traditions are taught and everything at Mountain Thyme is authentic. It is not a place for ego, it is a place to find yourself and work towards a better understanding of this World, the past World and the World of tomorrow.

Hannah is a true devoted ambassador for truth of nature. She has a wide experience of all ways of spirituality and traditional ceremonies, in fact a tremendous respect for the ancient ways and appreciation for the spiritual energy that the earth holds. She connects with all levels of nature, from the two legged, the four legged and the winged ones, a truly special lady, who has the insight into the World of Spirit and ancient ways. We talked for hours enjoying a mutual understanding, I consider Hannah to be one of my closest friends and we are of like minds. We were brought together for a special reason; this is now happening, for it is the time of the opening of vortexes of energy and healing. Only Spirit knows when and where it is to happen.

One night we had been channelling together and working with trance. Spirit said that her gift of trance was like a flower ready to open and sure enough it did when we were together.

It was my privilege to witness, 'The Bear'. This particular night something happened to me, I still marvel at it. I assure you I had not been drinking I was relaxed and the energies were so strong Spirit was waiting and then in trance I was told of three visions I was to witness. Again I repeat, I was completely sober and of sane mind, I was told that Spirit were going to show me the first vision that night and to remember it well.

I went to bed that night wondering at my sanity. I had seemingly dropped off to sleep when I was brought to my senses by a terrific bump at the end of my bed. I could not believe what I was seeing. It was the biggest black bear one could imagine, he looked at me and I thought my God I need my eyes testing, yet I was not afraid. He seemed to weigh me up, then just disappeared. My first reaction was to pinch myself and then check the doors. No one could have got in or out, not of the earthly type for certain.

Next morning I felt reluctant to talk about what I had seen as I could not make sense of it, then on thinking back, who am I to challenge? I know clearly I did not dream it. I saw it; I believe the bear represents the Earth and the energy of life, what next?

True to form next night I went to bed really wondering. No sooner had I settled when I heard the rustle of wings and a light so different filled the small room. What would I see and of course how disappointed I would be if nothing happened? Well I assure you I wasn't; this was an awe-inspiring sight, for before me stood a very strange figure. It was half man, half bird. He had the body of a bird and large wings yet the face of a man and the nose was a beak, resembling something from Greek mythology which is what I imagined it to be. Not a word was spoken yet his eyes were piercing into my very being. As soon as he came he disappeared. Since then I have been told it represents the eagle-dance. Again I remember thinking to myself am I round the bend? Most elderly ladies dream and hope for the vision of a six foot Italian with plenty of hump, well I didn't dream it neither did I get the good looking vision. What I saw was not of this world, in fact not of our time, yet a time of mystery and confusion to myself. The next morning I explained to my friend Hannah what I had seen. She did not seem as surprised as I had been and I felt at a loss to explain myself.

Again my vision did not speak with me and this left me perplexed as to why it had come.

The third night I was getting a little cross with myself wondering what I was supposed to do. Was I supposed to speak or acknowledge? Truly I was in a tizzy and none the wiser. Just very tired and mystified.

On the third night I was awakened from a very light sleep, and lo and behold there was not an inch of room not glowing in light. A huge figure stood facing me. As I sat up he smiled, then he spoke saying:

"Do not be afraid daughter you have nothing to fear from me, for your World and mine do acknowledge each other. I have waited long to speak to you, you are a daughter of the seventh plane and I salute you, when it is time we will talk again have no fear, I come in peace".

He was as tall as the ceiling with pure white hair that curled at his shoulders. He wore a breastplate of silver yet his legs were not covered and he wore a type of sandal with straps. His eyes were so blue they were like blue sapphires. He smiled, raised his hand, greeted me and was gone, yet the room was electrified with pure energy, I have once thought I caught a glimpse of him since, yet I am not sure who he was. That is something for me to know at another time.

Too soon my trip was over and I had to leave for home but not before I visited a amazing place called Turtle Hill. I am sure this is where one of the vortex of energies lies where there is water. It is deep under ground, pure and healing water. It is an amazing source of energy; common knowledge in the spiritual way of thought. This water will show itself one day and will give so much healing to this World of ours- whether in my time I do not know. I do hope to go back to the Black Mountains one day. It depends on my health and if I can fly, I do mean by plane! It is another challenge for me to go that far at my time of life. God only knows the mind is eager, I pray that the body will allow it.

I do know that the Indian way is good and it brings back the philosophy of old traditions, two legged beings for winged ones and the eagle energy. Is this man beast and bird? For these three represent nature, living and spirituality. Time will tell. Maybe I will go back in my lifetime, I hope so. I have great respect for the Native American who honoured the Earth and wasted nothing, respectful in their way of life.

The Wise One

The Wise old Indian Man,
Old man who waits and sits upon the hill.
He awaits his call,
In the distance he watches as the Eagle swoops flying
  high, free.
"Yes" he sighs, soon to be me.
He hears the night Owl calling, the owl seems to say
"Come grandfather come, come back to the hunting
  ground with me".
No more Buffalo roam in this special land,
The Coyote howls in the stillness of night.
All the old man's animal friends are free
He smiles to himself as gently, he rocks
Backwards and forwards, to the beating of his heart.
He gently sighs, murmurs "my land,
Is not as it used to be,
Great Spirit I am ready, I wish to be free.
To meet again my ancestors that is where I wish to be".
The breeze calls,
The stars light the way.
As the wise old Indian man, goes forward,
He joins the Spirits in the villages of yesterday,
This is his happy day.

Jersey

I have worked in Jersey for quite a number of years and find the place full of beauty yet a little wary of change. Maybe it's because for centuries they plodded on in their own way, and then came the invasions and everything changed. Still there are strong memories of the German occupation, mostly the bitterness has gone and people have accepted their past. Jersey was invaded and occupied by the German forces and all over the Island are reminders of that time. The community knew what it was like to be hungry in fact starving, yet still their traditions of working the land are paramount. In fact the Island is not only famous for its attractive tax regime but also for the potatoes and yet more so the tomatoes and the wonderful flowers that are shipped all over the World. With coming of the aeroplane, goods are transported much more quickly, thus making it a very prosperous island and a holiday place.

The main thing that struck me when I was sightseeing was the German hospital; it is an underground hospital building and has energy like nothing else I have ever experienced. I felt like a mole underground, trapped, cold and couldn't wait to get out. Historically it's well presented and its structure amazing still. It was built by a strong contingent of Polish prisoners of war and many other nationalities, it was forced labour and I could still sense the fear and deprivation of those times. When the German occupation was in full force the islanders knew hardship, I believe in a much stronger way than we did during the war years here on the mainland. It was an Island that had to produce its own food, there was nothing coming in and nothing going out. I understand the starvation was so great that there were literally no cats and dogs left. I pray that no one ever has this experience again.

Jersey has a very strong French atmosphere, whether it is to do with their past or not but there is almost a taboo against the likes of witches and what they represent, so when I first started my medium-ship there I was met with quite a bit of opposition. Now I can honestly say my demos in Jersey are received well and are very successful. I have also been asked to clear properties there which I have done and I also bless buildings, for their history sometimes lingers on within four walls and Spirits still visit old ground houses and memory spots. For instance at the old hospital I did see Spirit walking and I was told of quite a few young men who had been buried alive when there had been a cave in of the tunnels. In those days the German occupation held no sentiments and whatever food or medical supplies which the population held onto were confiscated . A lot of people left the Island before the occupation and a number of business men who were Jewish also left everything to find safety for their families.

I can remember one day walking along the edge of a cliff top and looking out to sea, I was aware that I was not alone; yes, I had the interest of a Spirit gentleman. He said he was Polish and he had been sent there to work, forced labour to be exact. He told me had tried to escape and was forced to work in the underground hospital and that he had been befriended by a Jersey family who had tried their best to feed him, yet they were starving themselves. He said after the war he married a local girl and had never left the Island - he had nothing to go back to Poland for, all his family or relations had perished. He had found peace and worked the ground belonging to his wife. He said that he, his lady and his children were buried in St. Martin's area, and he was happy, this was their favourite place. He still hated the dark and used to suffer long after the war from memories of the tunnels and the dirty work of digging underground bases for the guns.

He went on to tell me about the cruelty and degradation inflicted on the prisoners. Many starved and towards the end, the soldiers were also hungry. They were hated, however not all were bad and a lot of the Germans wanted to stay after the war on the Island. He kept saying "Ivan" then he disappeared just as soon as he came.

It was in Jersey where I met Ross and her family. Now please let me explain. Ross is a business woman who has a very shrewd mind and would not let anything happen or influence her decisions. Ross offered to help me with my tours. I was very grateful so we decided to give it a whirl. We travelled to Ireland - I can honestly say she knows how to organise things - I didn't realise how disorganised I was and still am today. Working together we had many laughs, we soon realised just how talented her son was and very open to Spirit, too open in fact, he attracted energy like a glue pot. I feel if he wishes, in years to come he will work in the way I work. I said to him as I say to anyone, medium-ship is different in all cases and one has to be able to close the energy off. This is not always easy and sometimes, even a very experienced medium we can be drained of energy. So again I repeat discipline is very important and responsibility to the client more so.

This talented young man accompanied me on many clearances and I know if he wishes he has the ability to continue. One never stops learning in this work and believe me I am no exception. I strongly believe in the power of Prayer and I trust my helpers in the Spirit realms.

Ross knew how to get people moving and how to organise. This shows in her own business. Some of the places we stayed in were strange to say the least; one particular cottage stands out in my mind while we were touring in Ireland. It was a typical Irish cottage of the past, primitive in many ways. Very cold, not good for me, I developed a very bad chest infection which turned to pneumonia. During one night I could not breathe so up I got so as not to wake the others with my coughing. I went downstairs into the lounge area and rekindled the fire. I felt as if I was being watched. I turned around and there stood an old lady with short dark hair pulled back in a bun. I noticed her small beady eyes, a cold looking hard women who clearly did not want me there. She wore a surged type skirt to the floor, I could see long sleeves and a shawl round her shoulders and a sacking type of pinafore. She looked hard at me, and asked me what I was doing in her house. Now at that time I felt too poorly to talk, yet I knew I had to explain that I wished her no harm and I would not harm her home. She said in a very grumpy voice, "You people come and go, you are not wanted". I explained to her that she was in a different time to me and I was visiting. She grunted and disappeared into the wall, I then tried to settle, but with not much luck as I was frozen. I finally dropped off to sleep, and awoke about 7a.m., aching in every bone in my body. Yes I had pneumonia and had to have an emergency appointment since I was in big trouble. Ross, John my husband and I struggled on. It amazes me that Spirit works wonders when I am to work for them. After the demonstration I literally fell into bed. Since then I have been left with lung problems at times and the old girl sometimes has trouble breathing especially walking up flights of stairs.

I was glad to leave that cottage, it was much too cold for me and the peat fire did not agree with my chest.

We visited a very old castle on our day off and I had a field day. Needless to say, the atmosphere was amazing. I saw wonderful Spirit energy and conversed with them. I was shown a tragedy of the past and a great number of true things that were not in the official guide. As I looked in one room I was aware of two dogs asleep in front of the fireplace that was a memory of the past. In another room I kept seeing a monkey, apparently he belonged there. So even animals show themselves and I never doubt what I receive from Spirit, yet it is the way you interpret it that is the link.

Judy, the dog

My mum and dad had a special little dog and her name was Judy. She was so small that she would fit into a good sized handbag. A character in all ways, when Judy was in the car you would not know she was there, mum and dad adored her, and in fact she was like a baby. If it was cold mum would wrap her in a blanket and never stopped telling her how she loved her. She would have the first cup of tea in the morning long before dad, often he would call to Judy, "Come along, tea time", and I remember thinking that one day that dog will ask for extra milk if it is too hot. She was a pure bred mongrel, yet as far as my parents were concerned she was a princess. On a Sunday the choicest bits of beef were given to her, and Sunday tea a choice of bread and dripping or bit of trifle. I know on today's animal diets many an eyebrow would rise; mum used to say they did not choose Judy, she chose them, she did well. When our children were small they were always taught to respect animals and so they grew up in harmony with her. During holidays Judy came to us and the boys loved it and I must admit I didn't want her to go back home. Then Judy's life changed.

Mum and dad moved into a ground floor flat where they had a little garden. It was not long before a nasty minded neighbour reported them to the Council for keeping a dog which was against the rules. In fact the dog was not as big as an average cat. My mum and dad were heartbroken, they just could not afford to move again as they had spent their bit of money making the flat nice. We all decided that Judy should come on an extended holiday to us, only until mum and dad could get a transfer to another house or flat.

I used to take Judy to see mum and dad and thankfully she did not pine for them. She had far too much to occupy her time as she always had three children happy to play with her. After a time we noticed she went off her food and we were worried. Ken, our second son insisted that perhaps she needed more cups of tea! I sensed the real reason, she was old and was passing blood, yes she had cancer. The vet was kind and I held her in my arms and she went to sleep. I was heartbroken, how could I tell my parents and since it was 9p.m., I decided to wait till morning before telling them. I thought, let them have a good night's sleep. Next morning we went to see them and mum promptly said that she knew Judy had gone to sleep as during the night both my parents felt her snuggle in the bed and kiss them. Even our loved animals come to say goodbye. I felt so bad about Judy's passing, yet as my mum said she was fourteen and we would not have wished her to suffer any more pain. We have never forgotten Judy and I know she is now well as I have seen her in my mother's arms.

Two years later my special dad died, we then lived in Wales. After the funeral I took some photos of the flowers on my dad's grave and sure enough there sat Judy, of that there was no doubt. She was with my dad awaiting mum when the time was right again. Just two years later my mother was reunited with them.

Stranger than fiction eight years later I was walking in Kidderminster down a road by the canal where at one time mum, dad and Judy lived. As I looked on the floor something glinted. It was a small disc belonging to Judy's collar. How many people had trodden that road in those years, why was it me who had found it? I started to think hard and remembered it was the anniversary of Judy's dying. I can honestly tell you that this is exactly what happened. I picked up the little disc and shed a tear and I still have it today.

When Judy came to live with us I bought a new disc as it was some distance from mum's flat yet the disc I found was the address from when they lived by the Canal. Animals are around us and the love of a human being for a pet is so special. I hope you like this little poem about a pet that Spirit gave me:

My Companion my friend

Where are you?

My house is empty
My heart is sad
I have lost the best friend I have ever had
He never asked for much a warm fire in the evening chill
A biscuit to munch.

The Postman's knock that gave him a thrill
From nowhere the scurry of four feet, the bark that did say
I know you are there come back another day
At all times a welcome for me, when back from the shops
    I came
His nose in my bag wanting to know where was his treat.
That was his favourite game
His welcome, worth more than gold
They say a dog is only a dog that's easy for others to say.
When my dog passed away yes I admit he was old and
    his tired bones would not let him play
Yet he was my friend in every way.
Always faithful my companion to the end.
We will meet again one day.
In a land where humans and dogs.
Can once more be happy and play
Yes every dog has his day

Young boy Robert

I remember once walking up to the town and a lady I knew was just at the side of me. Walking with her was Spirit, it was her son. He was surrounded with a fantastic light, a very special Down's Syndrome boy, I knew it was her son yet I did not know until that point that he had transcended to Spirit; he was 15 years of age. She moved nearer to me and said, "Margaret, can you fit me a reading sometime, I am so sad." I said, "I can't for three weeks as I am off to Ireland tomorrow, we will do it when I come back" She looked as though she would burst into tears. "Have you got half an hour now?" I asked. "We will go and have a cuppa".

We went into café, a small place and rather empty. I was glad about that though I don't think the manager was very pleased. "Will you accept a message from Spirit?" I asked. Her eyes filled with tears; she said that was what she wanted. I told her that I could clearly see Robert at her side. He had his arm around her shoulder and gave her a lovely kiss. She felt it and her hand moved up to her cheek. I smiled at her and asked her if she knew who that was; "I hope so," she answered, "was it my boy?" He said, "Mam calls me Robbie, tell her I love you, mam and thank you for the hanky you put in my bed". She said he was referring to his coffin. "I don't need it now, my nose doesn't run any more and I can sing, listen," he said. I must admit it wasn't melodious but that didn't matter, he was singing to her. I heard it but she sadly could not. He sang the Liverpool football anthem in a very loud voice. He said it was played at the funeral. She murmured, "Thank God my lad is safe." He had his Liverpool football shirt on and he and his grandad were having fun. He said his grandad was taking him wishing. She started to laugh. "Grandad always used to say wishing not fishing," positive proof of survival.

I left a much happier lady with tears not of sadness but relief. The café started to fill up so as always Spirit helped us; now they were going to help the café with business.

Then I rushed home to do my packing ready for Ireland.

The Belfray Inn

Let me talk to you about the Belfray Inn. The Belfray Inn is truly lovely, a good place where the guest is the important one and all the staff are so kind and helpful; needless to say the food is excellent. I met the owners many years ago while I was working in Jersey and we became good friends. They helped me to book shows and through them I found an extra family in Ireland, and I truly have found a genuine friendship with the family.

The owners Brian and John moved back home to Derry. They sold a very successful business to start back near their families. Jersey had been good to them and they were good for Jersey; this opened another chapter for them and certainly for me, and another chapter of my work.

They had bought a place that had been run down, for they both loved challenges, and once again they were close to their family. All was not well in those early days. The energy of the place was causing havoc, things were flying around, staff were a bit frightened at times and it seemed it was two steps forward, three back. That's when I started my work on the building. It is steeped in history and mystery and as I have said many times the energy that lingers is not always good, so I set to work.

Firstly, when you do this work you have to weigh up what has gone on before and why there is so much unrest. The only way is to talk to the energies of the past, call them ghosts if you like.

I found that the main problem was the surrounding ground, which had been scenes of fear, hardship, murder and sadness over a long period of time. Outside had been a well known Viking settlement that was holding energies, then there were fields where a long time ago there had been extreme fighting, many men had been ambushed, not forgetting a tree that was used for public hangings and being on the main Belfast road. There was much coming and going long before cars and like most places there was a stable where the coaches would stop to change horses. I heard distinctly sounds from the past of horses and the changing of the teams. That was no threat; it was a matter of understanding. I strongly say I do not worry about the dead, it is the living who would stab you in the back.

The difficult part came when I started on the inside of the Inn. I think it was the biggest job I have ever tackled. I started by cleansing and talking to the unseen residents. Some were stuck almost in their time yet encroaching on ours. To them, we were the intruders in their domain, so I began to tune in, by asking the help of Abe my Guide whom I trust, the angel energy and of course our God. I asked for their protection to see clearly and with compassion and to understand both sides of the situation.

Protection is the energy that I ask for to guard me against negative thoughts that do linger, also to protect me with angel light so that what I encounter does not leave me damaged in the way of negativity. The darker energy can play havoc with our field of thought so it is our responsibility to protect and I always ask for the love of God and the saints to be with me, and I pray that I always work for the good of Spirit and Earth people alike.

I ask time and time again, what does the Spirit energy want particularly if they are lost? I have moved quite a lot of confused Spirits into the light with no bother by concentrating on them and asking their loved ones to show themselves, asking the Earth-bound Spirits to join them as they were waiting and needful for them to take them, to guide them home. This happened about ten times, moving to the real cause of the problems. I started with the really troubled area, the cellars, stock rooms and the room where the electricity was. Electricity is a strong source of Spirit energy, and that area felt very oppressive. As I spoke with the Spirit energy I was told it had been an undertaker's workshop and bodies were kept there en route to the local churchyard, not always in the best conditions. This was the time of famine and disease many years ago, a time of great need for compassion. What did not help was that in that location were two ancient disused wells. I telephoned my special friend Jim who is famous for his clearing abilities, and he tuned into the area and the surroundings to clear the stagnant energy. The wells were both dry yet in the past they had been in constant use.

I was able to clear that part with Jim's help, then I moved to the stairs where someone, in fact a scullery maid, had fallen and broken her neck. I think the shock had kept her link there, once again she moved on and found peace. When I came to the store room all I could feel there was the Spirit within the bottles! My sort - sherry, wine and others, I did not do a stock check.

The kitchens were another thing; they were spotless and well maintained but much inhabited with the past. There were the old ways deeply engrained in the surroundings especially of the time when it had been a coaching inn. I saw an old lady plucking a chicken, she was sitting by what appeared to be and old fire place. To the left of her was a little lad who was turning a spit upon which a small piglet was cooking. I felt the intense heat of the open fire - then it suddenly disappeared. There was also another small lad, he sat in the corner just watching the fire - he must have been the 'odd job boy'. He was so thin and probably it was the only home he had known. I felt the activity, I felt the fact that the inhabitants could not understand the ways of the modern and they lived in their time World. I then explained to them they were fine, it was time to move on to join their families and friends in the Spirit World.

By this time I was shattered and ready for bed. Well, the soldiers of the past made a final move. I was just dropping off to sleep when the whole room came to life; no, I had not been on the bottle, neither was I entertaining. I felt the bedroom door come adrift and in marched a dozen men - 'wow'. In normal circumstances I would have thought it was my birthday. They marched through the room and out of the window. What I would have done then for a double brandy. That was the last time they were seen, they are at peace and calm and all is well.

After reporting the broken door the next morning, I had breakfast and completed the work in the dining room where sat an old Spirit woman who said she had a shop there, a teashop in fact, years ago and she was the old cleaner and the seamstress. Photos were taken of the fireplace where she sat and orbs were visible. The room now is totally different, very elegant and modern and our old lady has moved to a higher life or doesn't seem to stay in the new dining room. I decided to finish the work and investigated further the landings and bedrooms.

There were one or two rooms that were very cold with Spirit energies, one was the old sewing room and one a bedroom. After bringing in the light the atmosphere changed and warmth returned. The Inn is secure now. It is the most sought after wedding venue in Londonderry and is always full of clients. It is a happy place with entertainment, a very thriving business.

Ghost

Some days are strange,
My glasses disappear.
My purse is not where I left it,
Keys cannot be found,
The cotton rolls along the ground.
The door bell rings. No one is there.
Who hid my letter that was ready to post?
It must have been my friendly ghost.
I know he means me no harm,
Of this I have no doubt,
It is his way of showing he is about
When next he calls,
It would be easier for me if he'd shout,
Not move my things about.
Never fear my friendly ghost I wish not to shut you out,
If you are happy to visit me,
I am happy with your company,
If you are happy with mine.

Hauntings

I was visiting my friend's hotel, the Belfray Inn in Derry, the hotel which has played a very important part in my life. I had been doing a public demonstration. Very strangely my husband John and I were walking into our room after the demo and I heard someone say, "Listen, tomorrow you will look for the real people of the past, the very poor and under privileged of Ireland". I remember thinking, not likely, I am going to have a lie in, hasty words.

Too true, we went down in the morning and I watched other guests eating a full Irish breakfast. The plates were laden, the food looked so inviting. I was a good girl, I stuck to my fruit, toast and more toast, lovely butter to tickle my fancy. Just as we were leaving the dining room, from nowhere I picked up a leaflet someone must have dropped . I thought that's it, looking at it I understood the words I had heard the night before. It was about the Workhouse Museum.

This day was to be our free day; we ordered a taxi and asked to be taken to the old Workhouse Museum. We reached the place with no trouble, upon getting out of the taxi I felt very drawn to the building opposite. In the awareness of my third eye I felt such sadness yet I could see people queuing and having details taken. I saw them being deloused and scrubbed and they were left without pride. They had applied to come; it was the end of a sad road for them, the last resort, the final step of being victims of defeat and desperation.

As my husband John and I approached the main museum area, no one could fail to feel the misery and the feeling of rejection there. This is where I met at the door a very special gentleman with a friendly smile and we started to chat. He introduced himself to us, and said he was the local historian. His name was

Ken. John and I took to him straight away and he asked us if we were visitors to the area and we explained who we were. At that moment I heard someone say, "Hello, it's Margaret isn't it?" It was the familiar voice of a young man named Mark, whom I had met some years before when he was the presenter on a radio show, and he had interviewed me on the local radio station. He asked me if I would like to go live on air and talk about the museum as we walked around.

I did this gladly and was amazed at the energies that were still there, giving out such a strong feeling, you could feel the old vibrations. I felt the energy of the sad past, especially picking up on the people in charge of the workhouse.

The way they kept their records showed everyone was an item, an item with no individuality or no consequence. Men were kept separate from their wives and once a boy reached a certain age he was made to live as a man and also to work when possible. After all this was charity. Thanks be the works of charity have much improved.

We walked into the past, the past where the workhouse was the only means of shelter and where the only food was available to many, the last stop. After the first few steps I felt death so strong when I placed my hand on a large chest type box.

A Spirit lady said that she and her baby and others were placed in it after death then a mass pauper's burial was done; sometimes there could be 4 or 5 people in this box, sadly because half of them were penniless and ill; there wasn't much weight on them. There were slats where pieces of wood would be slotted in order to carry the load. The lady who was speaking to me had tuberculosis and she said her baby died during childbirth. She did not seem to be unhappy for she said she had joined her man in God's heaven where he had gone eight months before her baby was born. She smiled and said that they are now never hungry, are warm and are together with the other six children. What an existence to see your children die of scabies and fever. Thank God for the National Health service. We really know how lucky we are. It was a wonder anyone survived the workhouse, the last desperate place in a desperate world of want and disease. I will never moan again about waiting for my dinner, this was a lesson brought home to me that day. Thank God I know that my family will never be hungry, never know the humiliation of relying on goodness of charity for shelter.

We moved on to the sleeping quarters. Again I thought of my comfy bed and my warm duvet. The inmates had nothing, mainly straw palliasses and only rags or a type of clothing that itched, caused skin trouble and encouraged lice. Everyone was expected to share the work whatever it was. There was also a school room; nothing like ours today it would put me off learning altogether. I know there was a Matron whom I believe to be of a higher birth yet for some reason to do with her love life was working in charge of the workhouse, strange as it seems.

I smelt decay and fear, and utter desperation. What was most sad was the fact they had a rough material type of uniform, if they were lucky, and as soon as anyone died, strange how their few clothes soon disappeared.

As we were leaving this sad place I heard a child crying and I turned and caught a glimpse of the past again. It was a young boy, thin, ragged and carrying what appeared to be a tin mug. He was pale and his face was scarred with scabs, his hair was so thin, eyes like saucers, a vision of the past times, then he was gone.

Yes, sometimes the memory and energy returns to old places. I know he is at peace now, all is well.

Thanks be, those times are well gone and I do pray that Ireland will never have poverty, homelessness and famine again. Now Ireland is a different place and is progressing all the time, in fact a country of forward looking people. Myself, I find that I always receive a good welcome and I believe harmony is there.

Old Woman

She walked many miles, feet sore, belly empty
Crying out in despair, Lord can you not see my plight?
The winter winds wrap around her bony frame, faint
  with hunger and in the depths of despair,
Again she calls out louder than before, Lord what have I
  done to be this way?
My husband dead from fever,
My children lie in the pauper's grave,
Oh thinks she, what would I give for a place to rest and a
  crust of bread?

Still she struggles on to find her last hope, the Workhouse.
She may even for a night find a little warmth and
  somewhere to rest her head.
The snow falls; soon it covers the road where she has trod,
She hears voices tired and weary they ask in kindness,
Where are you going? To my last hope the workhouse she
  explained,
Their answer clear she did hear;
You have not a chance old woman, the queue is long
  and they have no rooms there today
We have tried and have been sent on our way and told,
  try another day.
Old woman sighs, tears of defeat run down her
  weathered cheeks.

It matters not she thinks, I have no more dignity,
She dropped to the ground remembering all her loved
  ones that are dead.
She burrows into the snow, starts to feel warmer but tired,
  no where to go, no one cares.

She sees a bright light, as though a thousand candles
  burn bright,
A heavenly sight, a figure so lovely so pure and kind calls
  to her
Come my dear, your family are here. She looks and looks
  again,
Yes from the realms of light her children call
Come mother dear, we are hear
With one last sigh, she joins her husband and children
No more hungry and lonely will she be,
Smiling she joins her family.

We were asked if we would care to visit more interesting places and without hesitation, said yes please, so Ken the local historian was our guide...

John and I drove in Ken's car to a very lovely old house. Sure enough it was occupied with this World and the next. It was a house used as a type of hostel. We moved around outside to find the old ways and sure enough I sensed a lady in a long dress carrying a basket. She seemed to have rose petals in it and I felt the years go recede as she glided into the house. We followed. She looked down at us from a top landing then moved to a bedroom. We went in and it was so cold, yet it smelt of lavender. I could see her standing at the window gazing outside; I felt her to be so sad, looking for someone. We turned back to the landing and I felt that someone had tumbled over the banister a long time ago. I knew there was a lot more energy to be investigated in the kitchen yet we could not go in as the house had visitors of the Earthly type. Perhaps another time, I hoped.

Again we were asked about a visit the next day to two other places, so we were picked up the following morning and had a mystery tour. We went to another large house, so different we did not go in just around the outside since it was a private, inhabited property. I would have loved to go in, but it is asking a lot for someone to allow you into their private home.

At this place we walked in the gardens and I felt a very uneasy feeling, knowing that in the past there had been much sadness. I distinctly heard children crying and shots being fired; it was more so by a wall where there were two big gates. I felt that there were bodies buried there and for some reason the pigsty was a place of fear.

I knew there was the energy of political problems and strong religious conflict also of rebels that hid in the grounds. Certainly there was a feeling of extreme unrest and in the grounds, which were large, there were no birds singing, which was more obvious by the wall and the gates. It would be interesting to go later at night; if we had we probably would have broken our necks. There was certainly a group of people and children who had been shot against the wall. The feeling was very uneasy.

The next place we went to was a field, a weird field one might say and I was asked what I was picking up with the energy, to which I had to say – nothing. That was until I got out of the car and my feet were firmly on the ground, then it was like a story being unfolded. I heard an aeroplane coming over very low. I felt it clip the trees at the end of the field and I saw that it was a plane of the 1st World War vintage. The end of the plane was broken in flight whereupon it nose-dived into the ground. I felt that there was mist there as it hit the earth. I clearly saw it explode, the pilot could not have stood a chance. Then I saw him. He said his name was Johnny and he didn't feel anything, he told me he had lost his face with the impact of the crash and also his foot yet his complete body would have been burnt. His helmet seemed to be made of leather, very close fitting. He wore what seemed to look like knee-high boots and his trousers were what I thought looked like riding breeches. He had a scarf round his neck and was very debonair and good looking. He said he was twenty-three and that he was with his mother in the Spirit World and she had found his death hard to accept – what mother wouldn't? I asked him about his lady friends and he replied, grinning, "Two special ones - one in Ireland and one at home". He said his home was in Kent and he had a brother and sisters. I felt he was the apple of his mother's eye.

Ken the historian asked me to ask him if he still come back much to the field? He told me he preferred the barn, the barn being and where the planes were stored and where he had also been seen. What a smashing good looking fellow he had been. He saluted us and returned to the ether.

The wedding blessing

It was my great pleasure and honour to be asked to do a family blessing in the Belfray Inn last January, a day to remember, a family time. My husband and I had a wonderful time with the Blessing, the champagne, the fantastic meal, firework display and the entertainment of a cabaret of the highest standard, as only the Belfray can do. It was a party I shall never forget. The ceremony was from the heart and it really made everyone so very happy and united.

Marriage is a declaration of love between two people and asking the congregation to witness the same. I usually ask the bride and groom to light a large candle at the start of the ceremony then the vows are reaffirmed by each person. Holding hands is so important and the groom usually gives the bride a red rose for love and she also does the same. Then they are blessed and a prayer of thanksgiving is said and the couple is showered in rose petals as a sign of gifts from heaven, the flower is living energy. The families give each one a flower token and applaud the happy couple. The vows the couple exchange are promises of continuing love and we ask those of Spirit to celebrate with us.

Paula

Paula was close in the family links of our adopted family in Ireland. It was strange how my contact with Paula came about. I felt as though we were friends yet we had never met. When I first was in touch with Paula it was through her special partner Rhonda.

Paula was dying, she had a very bad form of cancer and life was filled with pain. We would talk on the phone. I understood her pain because I have been there and as the saying goes 'worn the T-shirt'. Thankfully I was able to be of some help knowing what I know. I could help Paula with my knowledge of the Spirit World and life everlasting. I knew another member of the family Ronnie was watching over her and I know that he would be there for her, when the time was due so I was able to help in my own way. Still I feel so grateful to have been adopted. As Paula's illness grew worse and time was running out I would explain to her about the passing over and that there was nothing to fear, also the fact love cannot die.

I went over to Ireland and attended the funeral, it was a sad time and bitterly cold. The church was freezing and I think at those times one feels the cold more. When it came to the interment I chose to stay in the car and send my prayers in private. As the family emerged from the car I was told to tell them to look for the light. That is what I heard Spirit say. Sure enough on the family's return to the car I was told of the beautiful light that came down across the grave; I knew it was a blessing. What did cause a giggle and I thought typical of Paula's sense of humour at the final commitment, was that the priest gave the blessing for Rhonda and not Paula, her partner who had gone to Spirit. Perhaps, I thought, was it the cold or the Spirit within?

Since Paula's transition to the other side of life, I have seen her; she is well and free from pain. She watches over the people she loves, I do believe she always will - a poem for Paula.

The Angel came

The Angel came for Paula.
The Angel held out her hand
Saying "There is nothing to fear"
"Come Paula my dear,
I will be with you as forward we go,
No more pain no more tears"
You are Free"

Paula's heart is love,
Love cannot die.
Our tears are for us, the pain is still there,
The sharing of a joke,
The tenderness of a smile,
Nothing can take those memories away.

Me and my husband, John ready for a demonstration at the Radisson hotel, Jersey.

Demonstration in the Radisson, Jersey.

The Belfray Inn,
London Derry.

Demonstrating at
the Belfray Inn.

'Question time' live radio session, Ireland.

Hannah's Indian mountain retreat. Mountain Thyme, the Black Mountains, North Carolina, USA.

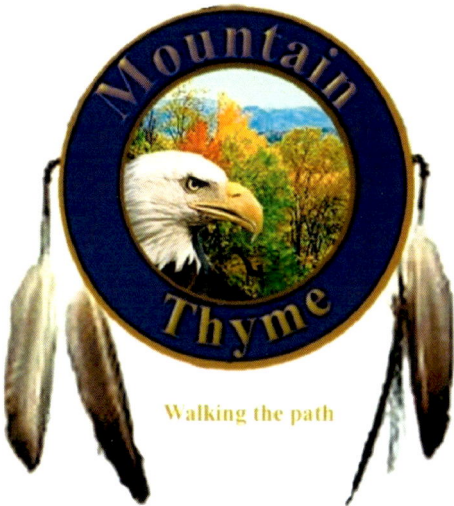

Walking the path

Patrick Guiney

Wedding blessing.

Donovan, me, James, Jess, Linda and son
with the vibrations of music.

Patrick Guiney

A tribute to a very special son missed by his brother Jim, sister Laura, brother Daniel, sisters Susan and Martha and a much loved granny Roseanne. Gone yet not forgotten, all who knew him loved him, his family hold him within their hearts, his treasured memory.

One of the strangest incidents that has happened to me was during a tour, when my friend Brenda was travelling with me. She was such a support, but then her husband became very poorly and our journey time had to finish. Brenda and I are still best of friends and try as often as possible to get time for our chats and coffee and of course the Chinese meals. We both liked our touring together, it was a good social life meeting really nice people.

Brenda and I decided to make the most of our free time in a very posh hotel where we were staying, Brenda went to the sauna and I went for a shoulder massage.

The young lady settled me comfortably on the couch and began to work on my very stiff shoulders; my shoulders seem to hold all the stress with me. So there I was relaxed and enjoying peace, warmth and comfort, a little bit of bliss in a busy schedule. I seemed to doze then I was brought back to the present, I sensed a young male of Spirit standing at my side.

He said to me very clearly, "Will you tell my mom I didn't do it, tell her I love her and my dad, all my family are so special, why would I do anything to hurt them?" The young man's Spirit was so persistent, he said his name was "PATRICK". I did promise, to the best of my ability that I would try to help. I asked the reflexologist if she knew of a boy named Patrick in Spirit, at which the young girl gasped and looked a bit frightened. I couldn't blame her really, she must have thought this is a queer one, this old bird is nuts - has a massage and talks to the Spirits.

Well, she confirmed she certainly did know the young boy I was talking about, it was her cousin. I explained that I had a message for his mom, the young boy was concerned about their sadness and worry and wanted to tell his mom and all the family that he was fine. I did say to the young girl if Patrick's mom wished to phone me I would give her the message myself. That seemed to make the young boy happy. Later that evening I received a phone call and was able to give positive proof of the young boy. I did not think I would hear from Patrick or his mom again but how wrong I was. I was demonstrating two days later, and a very persistent lad bounced in, saying "My family is here", he was so happy.

So strong was his energy, young and vibrant yet so loving, yes it was Patrick again. What a good looking young lad, a lad any mother would be proud of. He promptly encased her in lovely spiritual colour. It was very emotional even for me, when he said, "Please tell my mom I am okay, I did not take my own life, had no reason, everything was working fine for me". He kept on saying that he didn't take his own life – he wouldn't do that as he knew how much it would hurt his Mum. He said he had been at a gathering with another mate. They parted company at the door and he started to walk home to where he was staying with friends of the family. Suddenly three youths ran after him in a strange way as though they wanted his attention. He wasn't sure about them so he took to his heels and ran; he said he knew one lad, the others he knew vaguely.

Patrick kept talking about ginger hair and the other two youths being coloured. He did not return home to his lodgings that night and was found hanging in a tree later. Yet the belt he was hung by was someone else's belt. His was never found, that fact speaks volumes in the mystery. Also the previous night another young boy had had trouble. I think Patrick's death was a prank that went horribly wrong. He had a bruise on his head and from what he said he was dead before he was hung in the tree.

Naturally no one came forward, they would be too afraid. One day truth will come out and those responsible will have to come to terms with what they did.

Strangely I understand from his communication that he must have recognised his attackers. He was a brilliant sportsman who enjoyed life and had just successfully had an interview for a good job. The world was his oyster. This happened in America and the family live in Ireland. I can honestly say they are so much a loving family close in every way and devoted to each other.

My heart cried for Patrick's mother, I could not imagine the sheer hell for his family, how would I feel if it were me, could I cope? I pray that I could; only God knows my sons are my thread of earthly life. I thank God for my knowledge that life continues long after death. I know that this sad family gained their comfort from the proof of survival. No, they will never hold him again, yet thanks are that his family was able to bring his body home and their final farewells were in their own home, amongst the people he loved.

There are times I know when the old questions are asked. Why is it the good people who seem to suffer? Why did he have to be in a strange land when this sad thing happened to him?

The strength and consolation is they have not lost their faith or their son and as the rest of the family grow up so the united bonds strengthen. For they know that one day they will all meet again, all pain and hurt will ease. To the family he is still around them and his love is felt.

Love can not die, only the body, the real person is the soul. I know he is at peace and bears no hate, an inspiration to his special family.

It has been my pleasure and honour to keep in touch with the family; I thank God for being in the right place at the right time for the proof of survival given to me for the family.

After the demonstration I spoke to the family and again Patrick said, "Tell them I have met my other Gran Maureen from across the road and her sister Lily and the little ones, and of course my friend Gareth". He also spoke of a Baptismal font that would be in his little church and a commemoration Cup in his memory.

Love never dies. Neither can time erase the memories of a smiling happy face.

Our Patrick

The road ahead, seemed bright
We had to let you go
With tears in our eyes
With heavy hearts, we said our goodbyes
Our love was with you
As you journeyed to a foreign land.

Full of hope your adventure began, a new job
Everything to look forward to
Our boy was now a man
Then the world turned upside down for us
We were told that you, our precise son and much loved
*   brother had died.*
In strange circumstances.
That was what was hard to understand,
Things and happenings were not as said.
Truth was not told neither will it ever be.
This we understand nothing on Earth will bring him back,
We are now left with memories.

The laughing boy
The young man no more would we see
Our faith kept us sane

And our belief in eternity.
Hearts heavy, tears many
Patrick finally came home.
To rest a while with us while we said our last goodbyes,
A family together in grief.
Yet united in love.

Thank God nothing will ever hurt him again;
No one will be able to cause him pain.
He was too good for this World, to kind these are the
*   memories that he left behind*
A loving son a devoted brother the best in every way
He was the sunshine that kissed the clouds away.
In God's Heaven he is safe
Nothing can take the good memories away.

Our Patrick would not leave this world voluntarily
Fate decreed the way he died.
We will always know.
That he did not take his own life.
He has told us so
One thing is for sure
No one will ever hurt him again.
Love will never die.
We know one day in God's good time
Together again will we be.
A complete happy family

The twins

About twelve months ago I had a phone call from a lady who I had seen before asking for some help, also asking if she could bring her daughters with her. I never remember what I say to anyone and I couldn't remember what I had said to this lady. I was about to say, "I'm sorry, I'm not taking any bookings at the moment", when a gentleman stood in front of me and said, "Please, please help them, they need to talk," so naturally I did a turn around and said that I would see them two weeks later.

I usually do not like sitting with anyone except the person and a direct contact with the deceased, as one's energies can get pulled in many ways.

Anyway, I decided I would sit and went ahead. When they came the gentleman I had seen previously was around, he knew they were coming and certainly wanted to get his five shillings worth. He was obviously the husband, father of the group, and after talking to them of general things, he then proceeded to talk to them each one individually. He referred me to one of the girls. "Tell her I was at the wedding, tell her I saw everything and tell her I thought she looked beautiful, and that she should bring you a piece of her wedding cake". It's not very easy to tell someone can I have my cake. She confirmed that she had been married two weeks previously and yes she had brought me a piece of wedding cake. I then asked her to look at the photos of the wedding and there was an unusual face manifesting itself, and yes, it was her dad.

He then went on to talk about the other daughter. He had a laugh to himself and said jokingly that "she was in for a huge surprise". She had arranged to see an adoption agency in a week's time who would view their home and vet them. He said to her, "You won't need that, you may at a later date but you will be holding a baby of your own in nine months time". She said that they had seen every specialist available and have been trying for a baby of their own for 9 years and had given up. He said, "Not only one, but you do remember the twins in the family"' and they went out of the house saying, "That would be wonderful but..." He then turned to me and said, "The day the babies are born I will be there for another celebration, waiting and I will have my shoes blackened and polished". He then blew each one of them a kiss and was happy. True to form three weeks after her visit the young lady rang me up, couldn't believe what she had been told, and the doctors had confirmed she was pregnant. One very happy lady, and I said to her, "You will be ringing me up again in four weeks time", to which she replied "I will keep you informed". Well she did ring up and said she was having twins, and how I blessed her dad for I believe he was so happy to be able to give this news and for them to receive it.

Now the babies are five weeks old, a boy and a girl and all is well. The other point her father made was that the day the children were born his regiment, the Coldstream Guards, were given the freedom of the city. That's why his shoes were blacked. Spirit are wonderful.

Here is an article that the young lady wrote for the PSYCHIC NEWS about this experience;

'I would like to tell you about an extraordinary experience which my family and I had with a wonderful Medium named Margaret Hurdman. In order to do this, it's important first to explain a little about myself and what my family have experience during the last two years.

In 2005, we were given the devastating news that my dad had cancer. This was not the first time he had been diagnosed with it, but the doctors had been able to remove the tumour successfully on the earlier occasion. However, to be told that our dad had cancer for a second time left us shell-shocked as a family. We were informed early on that there was no cure for the type of cancer he had, and that surgery was not an option. Instead, my dad volunteered to be part of a clinical trial for a specific drug. This drug discouraged the growth of the cancer, but had side effects.

My dad continued to fight his debilitating disease courageously. The on the 2nd November 2007 he lost his battle with cancer. My mum had become a widow at just 48 years old, and my sister and I had lost our dad.

I was pregnant at the time, and due to the stress of the situation I had a miscarriage and was told that I would never be able to have children.

My mum was told by a close friend about Margaret Hurdman and the many people who had gained comfort from her readings. As a family we decided to visit her to see for ourselves.

On meeting Margaret we were instantly impressed. Very early on in the reading it became clear that this was someone who was extremely gifted and who did not make a living out of her gift. We feel that she is genuine in her desire to help people find peace and comfort after the suffering caused through the loss of a love one.

Margaret was able to communicate with our dad instantly. My sister had just got married and at the church wedding I had read a religious piece. Margaret was able not only to tell us that this event had taken place, but also to recite the words of the reading I had given. She named my husband as well as my sister's new husband without any prompting from us. We could not believe what we were witnessing.

Margaret continued by talking about the relationship between my mum and dad, and the precious times they had shared, giving details of which not even my sister and I had been aware before that day. Her phenomenal accuracy made our hair stand on end. Amazingly, she was able to pinpoint the specifics of my dad's illness as well as his final cause of death. As further proof that she was communicating with him, she began to recite the conversation my mum had had with my dad the night he passed away. By this point the three of us were very tearful as it truly felt that our dad was in the room telling Margaret his life story.

Margaret then focused on more recent events and informed us of what was to come. She did this by referring to the miscarriage I had suffered two years earlier. She also knew that my husband and I had been enquiring about adoption that very same week. Margaret was adamant that I would hold my own baby, despite the fact that I had been told by two top consultants that I would never conceive naturally. When I asked how she knew this, she told me that my dad was telling her that "the twins are coming back".

At this point, Margaret wanted to know if there were twins in the family already. My mum told her that my grandmother had miscarried twins, a fact which my sister and I were aware of.

At the end of the reading, Margaret blew three kisses at my mum, my sister and me. This was a gesture my dad would often make to us. It sent shivers down our spines, as again it was something she could not have known about.

We spent our entire journey home talking about how amazingly accurate Margaret had been. We were also intrigued to see how much of what she said about our future would come true. Four weeks after the reading with Margaret, I found out that I was pregnant, just as she had said. Furthermore, when we went for our twelfth-week scan, my husband and I were informed that we were having twins. Instantly everything Margaret had said came flooding back to us.

Since that first meeting, we have kept in touch with Margaret and have gradually informed her that everything she told us had come true. Our friends are amazed at how much of what she said has actually happened, and they are very keen to meet her themselves.

I would like to end by saying what an amazing woman Margaret Hurdman is. As a family, we have nothing but praise and admiration for her, and for all the worthwhile work she does. She truly is an asset to the Spirit World. We will never be able to repay her fully for the comfort and peace she has enabled us to feel. She truly deserves praise and recognition for what she does.'

PHYSIC NEWS, 23rd January 2010.

My special friend, Margaret

A Tribute to the memories of her past soldier love.

I have an elderly friend who is a very sweet lady, approaching her 90th birthday and I have the greatest admiration for her gentle ways and for her courage. I met Margaret when she visited Llandudno on holiday with her husband many years ago. It seems as though I have always known her. At that time I was a member of the local Lions Group, which is a charity organisation to help different causes and people; sometimes they help overcome times of trouble.

Yes, I did enjoy this voluntary work, yet as my medium-ship demanded more of me, time was short and I had decided that I would not be put forward for the job of community chairman again. In the meantime I had a phone call from a fellow Lion who had been staying with her in her hotel, a lady whose husband had been rushed into hospital and died. As this lady shared my interest of medium-ship it was thought perhaps I could help her, thus started our long friendship.

I visited Margaret and we got on like a house on fire if that could be the expression; during one of our many talks I was very aware of a young soldier who stood with her. He looked at her with a rare love, yet an innocent love. He told me that he was sunk aboard a ship during the war in foreign waters. He was a brave man yet, after surviving Dunkirk, another cruel blow was that the ship he was travelling in was bombed again and he was so looking forward to returning home to his promised lady to get married. He was not in the navy, in fact he was a fighting soldier. Margaret told me that the day when the news came, was like the end of the world for she truly loved him and still does to this day, nothing will ever change her first love. He was in his early twenties, a tall good looking fellow, and Margaret was small and dainty. Medals do not bring back love or heal a broken heart.

There is no grave to visit, no known resting place yet we know that he is in the eternal light and the love of God and that they will be reunited again some day. Then as we were talking her just deceased husband came through, saying he was sorry yet he knew he was not easy to get on with and he apologised. There were three men talking with Margaret - her late first husband and her recent husband, and the love of her life (Les), her soldier boy of her early years never to be forgotten. Then a little girl appeared. She was like an angel and blew kisses. She was the new born baby that had not survived childbirth. Margaret shed a few tears yet it struck me at that time and still I marvel how brave she is losing the love of her life and her two husbands. Life deals some people a lot of hard blows yet it is how we deal with them that matters. Margaret to me is an inspiration, and light to follow if one can.

Time went by and I kept in touch with Margaret and pray to God that she will have no more sorrow. I went to visit Margaret in her home in Telford. As we were having a cup of tea a young man of Spirit came in. He said he was Alan, Margaret's son who had gone into Spirit unexpectedly with what should have been a minor complaint yet he went home to God, which was a tragedy. He was a clever man and one thing is for certain, when Margaret ascends to a higher life what a wonderful time it will be for her, and a joyous reunion with her family, especially Les her young soldier love and Margaret's children who will be there for her. Then truly her life will start anew.

The Angel Child

I felt a chill across my shoulders,
I sensed someone at the back of me
Turning I did say "I know you are there,
What do you want me to say?"
A childish giggle could be heard far away.
I did say "Hello my darling have you come to play?"
The cotton rolled across the room,
The breeze lifted the curtains, gently they did sway
Then I remember the memories I had hid away.

It was four years ago this very day, when last we did play,
We picked blackberries, arrived home with laughter in
*   our hearts with flour everywhere, Fingers stained*
*   with juice,*
She did say "Aunty we are having fun today",
We baked a pie; we were so happy you and I,
This special Niece whom I loved so dearly.
Sadly that summer's day four years ago
Was our last baking day.

Now only ghostly giggles do I hear
You closed your eyes,
The Angels came and carried you away,
They look after you as you happily play,
Especially in the summer months
When the blackberries bloom,
I remember the loan of a niece, who loved to play,
She took my heart away.
She was too good to stay,
Only loaned to us on Earth
A short time to play.

Simon

I met Simon when he was in turmoil about his life. I can honestly say he is one of the kindest, nicest, caring people, and it has been my privilege to meet him.

He came to see me a week before going into hospital for major surgery. Spirit gave me an insight into himself. They did show me his aura, which was undertaking an upheaval and I picked up bad headaches with him; no wonder, the surgery was for a tumour on the brain.

His concern was not for himself it was for his daughter; you see Simon was divorced and he adored his child. He showed great courage and great spiritual insight and as we talked his father came through, from the other side of life and said he was sorry that he didn't spend more time with him when he was alive and yet he was very proud of Simon and his brothers. The other two sons, very different from each other, were very talented young men. Simon was an exception; yes, talented, and very understanding of life. He did show me his CV, which was with the police and with that he should have risen to the top of his field. He was very trusting which is not easy when you're facing a life changing operation. True to form, Simon went into hospital and received his treatment almost immediately. It was touch and go yet Spirit already had plans for him, not in the Spirit World but on the Earth plain. The tumour was removed and he was on his way to full recovery. Before he entered hospital I was shown that his understanding of people would lead him further into knowledge of the earth plain and that he would be sitting a major exam when he was strong enough, which he did. Spirit showed me a certificate; this would be the final of the exam and all of his studies.

Two years on he is a Chief-Inspector who gives so much to this World and I know will continue to do so. I felt that his life was a gift to others and Spirit had their purpose in his life yes a truly lovely man with a great spiritual gift and a pleasure to have met him, In fact a lovely family.

All through Simon's time of trouble, he was receiving healing from the church groups and from Jim my friend, who is a very sincere power of healing. Simon is now perfectly clear of the tumour and his life has been given back. He now will live the life that he was meant to live.

Road, sea, air and two feet

When I have finished a demo I am usually very tired. Once I have eaten, all I wish to do is sleep, more so than 10 years ago. That I admit could be age or could be the energy and feelings were so much stronger with no half measures.

Usually after finishing a show my feet are killing me and my back feels as though it is just on a different planet. I cannot sit during a demo or work. I have to keep moving around, that is the way Spirit and I work best together, on the move. I can honestly say when I go on stage, I must be comfy, in fact wear nothing too tight especially on the feet. My mind must be receptive to thoughts, smell and vibrations for all these are signals to the mind and the channels will open doors, listen and we hear, listen to hear, do not turn your back on the wisdom of the years.

Going back to the original title of this part, Road, Sea and Air, sometimes travelling back after a show I am not completely closed down and because of the high awareness one is more receptive to surroundings

One particular night in the car we were motoring over a mountain road. It was misty and rather dangerous when suddenly a man walked from nowhere in front of the car; well it frightened the daylights out of us. I can remember saying to my friend who was driving, "We have bloody hit him," and more choice of words. There was no bump, and I had not been drinking. We got out of the car, it was 12.45a.m. and there was no sign of anyone. We called out, and saw nothing, the mist was getting thicker and how can you report an accident that wasn't, so we continued on much shaken.

I wrote the facts down on reaching home. Next morning I rang up the police and explained, saying it could have been a sheep, yet I didn't think so. The policeman took the details and said that the same thing had been reported many times before. I honestly thought he was taking the mickey, yet later on I found out at that precise time this scene of the past shows itself, and it still does. I don't drive that way much these days.

One of the funny things that happened to me was when I came out of the theatre one night half asleep, I opened the car door, got in and turning to my mate said, "Gosh I am tired, are we ready?" The reply came, "I am if you are". I was in the wrong car! How the driver and his friend in the back seat laughed – that's all we could do. I was full of apologies to which he replied, "Well lady, I said I would like to meet you at the show so be it, I never thought it would end up with you and me in the front seat together".

Another funny incident touring, was when we were stopped for a spot check, and the officer asked where we were going and what for. So as we told him, he looked strangely at us, laughed and said, "Well, that is the best laugh I've had all night, are you telling the truth?" so we showed him a poster. He asked where we were next working and said he would come to the demo. He did with his wife and son, so as you see all travel is not boring.

As I mentioned in one of my previous books about the time when we unwittingly parked in a cemetery gateway, we were in a camper van and halfway through the night my friend was snoring so loudly it woke me up. Then I heard a funny sound. I looked out of the window and a lorry driver was peeing just outside the van. My mate gave one big snore and he moved so quickly I don't think he finished his task. Then the next morning we realised where we had parked - outside the cemetery entrance. I bet he thought the dead were noisy.

My friend and I were returning from Holyhead after doing service when we saw a man sitting in the middle of the road. I remember saying, "What the hell is that bloke doing?" We braked and again there was no one there. What we saw was definitely not an optical illusion; apparently a young man had been drunk and sat in the main road, twelve months previously, and had been killed instantly by a lorry. He has been seen many times yet he seems content to be there, sad isn't it? It was his intention to commit suicide. All I can say is God help the driver of the lorry. He has to bear the burden of guilt yet there is none as it was unfortunate that he was where he was at that time.

The church

I was invited to do an interview for TV and I thought 'great', so off I went from home in Wales, stayed the night in a B&B and was picked up next morning by my friend Brenda who came with me. I thought we were on our way to the TV studio so I was very surprised when we drove straight past the studios. I asked the taxi driver, "Excuse me, are we in the correct taxi?" to which he replied, "Yes, we are booked for the church." My reaction was Blimey, what's going on! We arrived at our destination where a young man was filming outside a renovated church; it had been turned in to a very classy modern pub. I was then introduced to a young guy who explained that this is where we were filming. I was gobsmacked, if I dare say the expression.

We were shown around the place and I must admit I found it a hive of activity, Spirit sought not the bottle as the pub was still closed, and this was a treat to work in. Not being entirely sure what the crew wanted I just went with the flow. It was an interview about me and my journey back from death and the start of my medium-ship. Soon the pattern changed for I could feel and hear past Spirit energy talking to me. I could see things and happenings of the past. I was told about the graves that had been dug up and still the pub had visitors of the past frequenting the place. I saw a couple of soldiers at the far end and saw where the old baptismal font had stood. I was transported back to the troubled times of Ireland and was shown where the vaults were and told how some had been filled in when renovations were made. I also saw an old man in the far corner, just happy to be there; no harm in him, he apparently was often seen. I was told of missing photos that had disappeared; they were photos of influential people of the time. Time went too quickly and the staff had to prepare for their day's work. There was a lot I would have liked to talk about yet time had run out on us.

The strange thing was I never saw the film, as we were soon on our way back to the airport to return home.

Yet through that interview started another important chapter of my life that was and is important to me.

Katie, Helen and Paul

A few days after arriving home I had a phone call from a young girl who sounded so vulnerable and she asked me if I did private sittings, as she had seen me on TV.

I was just about to say no when clearly my friend and Guide Abe said, "Yes you will". I heard the name "Paul" called to me and asked the young lady if the name meant anything to her, thereupon she cried. I felt the energy that was talking was a very new Spirit, yet the energy was of an older man and he had no difficulty in communicating with me. I now understand why, yes it was Paul her dad. I continued to talk to her, and asked if she would like to speak with me later as I was due to go for a blood test. I said I would leave that up to her.

Well it was meant to be, that sitting started a strange beginning to a very social friendship. Paul was a very famous man, I did not know this at the time. He was the founder of the Paul Golden Clinic, a very special and highly thought of establishment which deals with so many problems and has the ability to help many. Yet Paul was continually repeating he was fine and he had no idea that he was joining the Spirit realms. I promised Katie and her mom that when I went to Dublin I would do a private sitting for them both. They had touched my heart, they were lost in grief.

I had no idea of Paul's importance as an entertainer .In fact he was and still is world renowned for his shows and demonstrations of hypnotism. He called his gift mind over matter. I have witnessed the influence he had by his recommendations, certificates and popularity with all types of people. He adored his princess, Katie, and she adored him, and the love that held his wife Helen and daughter Katie together is a very rare thing.

Paul had been married before and has sons who are famous in their own right. Every time I have communicated with Paul, Abe has always given him a Jewish Blessing which is nice, for Paul is and was a Jewish gentleman – nobody's fool. Devoted in his love for his family Helen and Paul I believe had a good life together and she, a brilliant organiser, managed his stage shows.

When I next visited Dublin I contacted her and from that day on they have filled a spot only for them in John my husband's heart and mine. When we visit it's like going home and I now have another granddaughter. Helen has opened many doors for me and I am so very grateful. I hope that I have helped them in my little way.

After visiting some time ago I left the house and suddenly Paul was at my side. I was in his drive and he gave me a few seconds for me to recognise who he was, even though I did not need them. He then said, "Do you have to go? I like my mouthpiece being here." A strange compliment yet I knew what he meant. I was quick to say I would be back and to assure him that I was always there for my extended family. We have had some good laughs, yet underneath our smiles I know how much they miss him, a special man who could make the world turn and calm troubled waters.

The strange thing was neither Helen nor Katie had originally seen the TV programme yet it had been recorded and it seemed as though it kept coming up on the screen. Until Katie rang me. I had known nothing of Paul Goldin.

Spirit know what they want and usually get it, it works in mysterious ways.

Shalom Paul.

When you are asked to describe your father

What could you say, what words would describe?
There are no words to say,
Why this special man and his memory,
Are never far away.
It is the little things that mean so much,
The funny little look that wraps around your heart,
The silly things he did that made me laugh,
The cheeky grin that lightened my day and the gentle
*   kiss good night,*
That chased my fears away.

When the time came for us to part that is what broke my
*   heart,*
My Dad a special guy who always had time for me
Even when tired, he would say, he loved me and never
*   ever chased me away.*
He taught me all I know.
Taught me how to love,
Most of all how to smile through a dark day.

All these things I know
Yet my heart cries out to my dad,
Why did you have to go?
In my sadness I still cry.
Dad I loved you so,
Yet I know for sure this is not the end
When I am old and grey, and have children of my own
I pray that their love for their father is like mine.
Nothing will ever take it away.

Music

They say that music feeds the soul; I know this to be so true. Have you ever listened to hard heavy music and found yourself depleted of energy, and thoroughly miserable? Then know this that type of music is not for you, for music is vibration, and we work within the vibration of the mind, the sound and the Universe. This is why a medium will hear the speech of Spirit in their mind, and very often an Earth person's voice can tell you so much about them. For example; a whining voice means basically a moaner, a person that gabbles and talks very quickly shows me they need to stop and listen to themselves, a high pitch squeaky voice proves to me a person that lives on their nerves, everyone's sound means something different to other people.

Donovan
When I talk of music feeding the soul, there is nothing better to release the energy of the mind and clear obstructing thoughts; it has been my privilege to meet famous musicians. One of these is Donovan, from the era of The Beatles, and flower power. He has an insight into young and old and had taught his gifts to others. He and his wife Linda both share the interest of Spirit and healing, he believes like I do that even the ground needs healing sometimes. When he plays he's on a different vibrational plain, they are both joyous to know, and we are so different as people.

James and Jess Hooker
James Hooker and I met during a demonstration in Ireland. Jess his partner like Donovan and Linda are free spirits, and they enjoy the ways of music and revel in healing energy. James has been very successful and produced some really good music, in which I have been allowed to share. James is a calming man, with what I would call a delicious voice. It never ceases to make me laugh,

and laughter is healing. We stayed with them in Majorca, what a lovely time. I used to send John out of a morning to pick oranges and lemons from Jess and James's grove; we made pigs of ourselves. I'm now quite a dab hand at squeezing oranges. We hope to be going again this year and enjoy the sunshine and Spirit with friends. Incidentally while we were there in Majorca, all of us went to a mountain area that is steeped in history and had much unrest. We worked on it together and cleared the energies that were not compatible. Incidentally James named his last CD after me: "Maggy's Drawers".

Chris de Burgh

I met Chris through his daughter, and my friend Helen. His daughter, Miss World, is named Rosanna, and what a beautiful girl she is. Chris and his family came to one of my demonstrations; we all had a good time after the show and ideas and interests were exchanged. I was privileged to go to Chris's home, the most beautiful place one could hope to see, private, family wise and full of good vibrations. He played for me, which I enjoyed thoroughly, for his music has a healing power of its own, it comes from the heart and speaks volumes to the mind. There is no edge about Chris, he is a true healer and I thank him and his wife for their friendship.

This is why I say to people vibrations are important to a medium, vital in fact as for without vibrations we cannot work. This is why I ask of my audiences to speak to me as a nod or a grunt will not do. When I feel Abe my Guide coming though it is with a high intense, piercing buzz, or if he is around me at any time I feel that noise, and is has been felt and heard by other people of like mind. It is the same with a phone, if you pick up the phone and you don't like the sound of the voice, you are automatically on your guard. To me that is awareness, and sometimes it pays to be aware of your own intuition. I also do play music quite often, when I'm meditating or needing to relax, for life can be busy and hectic and we all need a little time for ourselves.

Meditation

Ask yourself what is meditation?

I believe meditation is a time when you can be at peace and not worry about the usual problems. In fact meditation should give you the calmness to deal with your problems or at least to see them in a clearer way, thus helping you to find peace in your heart and mind and a feeling of relaxation. For me to meditate I have to be free of stress, one can not sit and relax if you know you have left the cooker on or if someone interrupts you. This is the only way I can meditate:

Turn the phones off, put a note on the door 'do not disturb'.

Clothing must be comfortable, not tight and of course avoid being cold at the same time. If you are too hot it can inhibit you.

A light airy room is a must and a comfy chair where you can put your feet flat on the ground and keep your spine straight. It matters not where you put your hands as long as you are at ease.

Different thoughts on meditation, feel either that the hands are placed together or upturned.

Some people have looked aghast at me when I say about positioning of the hands. I can't imagine me holding out my hands as once was suggested to me. If I did that I would never relax, I would end up with cramp.

Usually I play a little light soothing music which also helps the vibrations and the serenity of the room, fresh air is ideal not a full force wind, just what you feel comfortable with.

My next step is to listen to my inner silence, in other words accept that you are ready.

I strongly urge you to ask your helpers of the Spirit to work with you and not to let anything that is not of goodness invade your space. I call this bringing in my doorkeeper, visualise a trusted being who will protect you and look after you, bid them welcome

Next I ask for the angels to be with me and I say my own prayer. I am a great believer in the power of prayer.

In my own mind then I am ready.

I open the energy of my feet, bring up the energy up, up to the private area, up, up again to the tummy, up, up again to the middle of chest then up to the heart, feeling the energy and awareness building up again rising higher to the throat Chakra. Up, up again to the middle of the forehead, the third eye and up to the top of the head, the frontal area.

Visualise this beautiful white God - given energy cascading all around your body. If you feel easier by doing this exercise repeat it again until you get used to this state and confident.

May I suggest an easy meditation to start?

We will together sit relaxed, be with me.

I want you to imagine a lovely white cloud,

Sit yourself on your cloud, you are comfy, all is well.

Feel the warmth of a summer's day.

You are gently gliding on your cloud, you are safe at all times.

Are you seeking confirmation of something? Or do you wish to find peace and some tranquillity in your mind?

Ask yourself who would you like to see?

Enjoy this time, perhaps a memory of a loved one, the nearness of a much beloved pet or a time of peace to know yourself.

Relax, relax, listen to your heart, be aware of your needs, if you wish for guidance ask. Remember this is your private time and your thoughts are your own, do not be afraid.

Do not be afraid to seek the answers, your lovely white cloud that is allowing you this time is always there if you wish, it is your escape to finding peace so any time you need that time allow yourself to meditate. When you are ready feel yourself returning to your chair, step off your cloud and watch it glide away. You can at anytime go back on your cloud. It will take you at anytime you feel the need on a journey of your choosing. Remember if you can what you felt. Who did you see?

Now you are back in the now, feel your senses of your body, wriggle your toes, stretch, and thank your protecting angels and your helpers for being with you. I always suggest a drink of water, you can visualise your own meditations, dispel the fear of the unknown and be assured you will not be harmed. The more you are confident, the longer you will wish to sit.

Anytime you wish you can bring yourself out of meditation state, just sit quietly anytime you wish and you are able. Meditation is your time to find your inner peace. Do not forget to thank your guide, also the angels, and all the unseen helpers for the help and guidance you have received.

I remember in the beginning I found it very hard to meditate because I found myself planning the dinner or feeling guilty, that I was sitting when I should perhaps have been doing the ironing, I also found because I was relaxed I fell asleep during meditation startling myself with my own snoring. Don't feel guilty it is probably what I needed as so may you.

Everyone needs a time for themself, sometimes make this time and you will feel the benefit, discipline yourself to relax and find your inner peace. You will not regret it.

This is my method, you may prefer a different approach but that is up to you.

If you can find that little time for yourself each day that is good, also it is ideal if you can keep the same time. That is not easy, we live in a World in which we forget to find time for. ourselves.

Alan

One day, a few years ago I sat catching up on some paper work when the telephone rang. It was the SNU. (Spiritualists National Union) Now the SNU is basically the ruling point of many mediums, it is a organisation that securely holds the correct way of proceedings and is in fact the foundation that governs us as mediums, and is the centre of the correct procedures

Because I am registered with the governing body the union knew that I would do the best I could, only giving the truth.

This is a good thing because too often the World of Mediumship is abused and too many charlatans give the dedicated medium a bad name. We deal with people's emotions and at all times responsibility is a must.

I must admit I have come across so-called mediums who claim things and contacts that are not there. When this happens it makes me cross because we are often dealing with very raw emotion. This was so with the client that the SNU was ringing me up about.

The phone call was regarding a gentleman who needed help; they wanted my permission for him to contact me.

I remember thinking, do I want to read? Then without a second chance Abe, my Guide, came through and said, "Yes you will read", so (he that speaks will be obeyed) the wheels were put in motion.

Now I am not a nervous type yet an unknown gentleman coming to sit in my little room concerned me a little. When I concentrate in a sitting you are vulnerable to whom you are with. I basically felt that I needed some security. The gentleman in question would not even give me a name; I must admit this made me wary so I asked my husband to wait until the man arrived. I know

Abe would protect me yet still I was a little on edge as I had no idea of the purpose of his visit.

I live in a very modest bungalow. No expensive trappings, we are ordinary people and live a very ordinary life. The car drew up, it was a sight for sore eyes, luxury at the top. I went to the door to greet my guest a very smart distinguished man, with much class if that's the word.

As he came in I was aware of the Spirit world with him; there were three ladies. I knew it would be fine for John my husband to carry on and go shopping.

I offered a cup of tea. I had to use china, not the usual mugs, but he declined saying perhaps after his sitting. So we sat down and I asked him to relax feet firmly upon the floor, I call it grounding.

He was tall, and looked so sad, I spoke for a few moments telling him what to expect and he said he knew nothing of mediumship and if it would even work for him, he seemed a little doubtful yet full of hope. I also explained each sitting is different, and the results depended a lot on being very open, explaining that is not always the person you hope for that communicates, also that one Spirit will often bring in another.

We sat quiet, the room was ready so was I, then without further ado I heard a voice that I know to be Abe, my Guide. He said, "Tell him, Shalom my son, Shalom". At this point my client nearly fell off his chair saying that is why he refused anything to be known about him.

"I am a Jew, and I did not want anyone to know". My words to him were tough, Spirit are wiser than you think especially Abe my Guide and Helper. I said to the gentleman, "Spirit have respected our talk and acknowledge you". To this statement he smiled. When I explained there were three ladies with him, his words were, "I am glad".

I explained that one lady said she was his wife and had recently joined the Spirit realms, she showed me a lovely little blackbird resting on her hand, I remember thinking oh, Gosh, he will think I belong to the loony house. She said her name was Kathy and she had died of bowel cancer She spoke of many personal things with which he was delighted. Then she scolded him saying because he was so lonely he had contemplated taking his own life. He cried, yet he cried tears of joy knowing she was still around for him and watched over him and he confirmed that she did indeed have a pet blackbird that she had rescued and reared.

Then the very old lady spoke. She said she was his nanny of many years and loved him. She spoke of her wedding present to him of some old paintings, in fact Japanese on silk. He said they held pride of place in his lounge. In fact she had been like a mother to him. She was the only source of love as a child, no wonder he loved her. She related childhood episodes and said how his brother in Spirit was a naughty boy and could turn their parents around to his way of thinking; and how he had always been the favoured son and yet was a rogue.

In fact his nanny was very precise, this I related to him and it was confirmed.

The other lady made her presence known, she said she was his first love and she died of TB while he was serving abroad. She did not give her name, which I could not understand. I asked again and she giggled, apparently she liked to play tricks. My reaction was that when she was ready she would. What then came into my mind was a memory of my good friend of many years. Her name was Gladys, and sure enough that was the Spirit's name. This is sometimes how Spirit works and why one has to keep alert. We were still talking two hours later. John arrived home and I asked him to brew up.

I was by then ready for a cuppa and we sat chatting together. It was time for the gentleman to go, so he asked me what he owed me and before I could say anything Abe piped up, "No charge". I remember thinking bloody hell, yet I have to obey and respect the wishes of Spirit. I know often Abe says man is worth his labours but am I missing something?

The gentleman, whose name was Alan asked if he could keep in touch and naturally I agreed..

From that first visit a strange friendship was started with my husband, he was very understanding of Alan's ways and showed kindness and patience with him. Alan was not an easy person to understand. Always rather bossy yet that was his upbringing and we understood.

A few days later a registered package arrived for me. I couldn't think what it could be yet I noticed the lovely handwriting. Yes, it was a gift from Alan. A watch that had been his darling wife's and he had sent it to me as a gift, as he explained, he had no family and he would like me to wear it. Even as I write this I am wearing it.

We included Alan in many things and I helped him to understand spiritualism. He grew more and more aware and found peace within himself knowing his beloved ladies were around and had not forgotten him.

I remember once in his car, we had been to an opening of the owl sanctuary that he supported. He said it was strange that Kathy had never given him his pet name, to which I explained when she was ready she would.

He often asked me to visit the charities he supported and he told me and I understood that all his money was going to these charities, one being a trust to protect animals from uneasy suffering during research. As time progressed he became a firm believer in the spiritualist way of life and learnt much about the progression of the human soul.

One day we were talking about his childhood and Kathy drew close. She called a name to him and it was what he wanted to hear – his pet name for her. Better late than never.

He then became very ill and was diagnosed as having the same disease as his dear wife; he only wanted to join her. I understood this as life was not easy for him, a man who was used to being in control now being literally controlled by his illness. He used to say he could not wait to join his darling

I visited him regularly in the nursing home. I promised that I would be there for him at the very end, as I was.

I had only been back a couple of days from visiting and the phone rang. He had had a slight fall and was slipping farther away from this life. I took a taxi to Manchester immediately praying I would be in time. I was sitting at the side of his bed and he was mainly unconscious when an icy cold blow encased the room. I could smell freesias, his darling's favourite flowers. He gently turned his head and there were two lovely orbs in the corner of the room. He smiled a lovely smile and I heard the song, "We will dance in the old fashioned way".

That evening he was at peace with the ones he loved. Nothing more was to be done except the final arrangements, I had promised I would deal with those and I hopefully did as he wished.

I left the nursing home and was joined by his kind lady who had cleaned for him in the past. We went to his apartment and collected the clothes that he wished to wear, he was so precise in his instructions, and the personal things he wished to be with him, and of course the instructions for the final service. The music he had chosen and the CD to be played was his choice, "We shall dance in the old fashioned way". Apparently it was their favourite tune. They are now together and neither will ever be lonely again. Goodnight, God bless.

I have seen him twice since, each time he thanked me and John, my husband for being his friend, and also for the comfort that he gained in the spiritual's way of thought.

He gave his permission for me to share his story before he passed early this year 2010.

Loneliness

When the heart in despair cries out
Is there no one there?
No one hears
Where are you, are you there?
I call your name.
Silly me I am alone

All is quiet.
I see the empty chair where once you sat
The cushion neat and square
The noisy clock ticks away
Like my melancholy mind
If I stop the clock the silence will break my heart
Sending me into deeper despair

I ask again and again.
Please call my name
Show me you are there
Do I ask too much?
Learning to trust when you are lonely is hard to do
In my solitude I say every day is a bad day

Forgive me dear I would not wish you back to pain
You are free,
Nothing will ever hurt you again
It is me that cries not you.
Forgive my mistakes
I am lonely without you

You are free
I am chained by my wishful thinking
You are where I wish to be.
It is said that time heals.
How can this be?
My time is an empty shell

I am the lost one
Please do not be too long my love in coming for me
I pray we will sit together again;
We will laugh and be happy walking as we did.
Though the bluebell woods.
Or dancing in the old fashioned way.

I smell your perfume, I feel your touch
I remember the gentle touch of your hand.
Memories are all that are left to me.
Till my time is come, and we are as one
Never again to part, for you my dear are the other half of
*   my heart*

The end, but not the end

During my life I have been influenced by many people, perhaps sometimes trusting too much, again that is free will. If I could live my life again on this Earth of course there would be many changes. Like most people, as we grow older we see things clearer and often in more perspective. I would not say that I am wiser, I can only say that I have been given the insight.

Life is like a circle, it starts from a very small beginning, grows volume, grows in interest and the knowing that the life we have is not to be treated lightly, yet must be treated as a privilege. Yes, we come into this World with nothing, no clothes on our backs, we go out of this World with very little else, yet hopefully with the knowledge of a certain life to come.

It is how we treat people in this World that makes us what we are, who we are, why we are. I do believe on the day that I am called to a higher level. It is my conscience that I am answerable to, for all the deeds and the un-deeds that have crossed my path.

If I have been of use to anyone I hope it is for the good for the knowledge that Spirit has given me was to be shared. In the course of my life I have doubted, for I am human, and there are many times when I have said, "Why me?" Yet I know the pattern of my life was set for me, I pray I have used my life with understanding to give hope, to give love to people who need to know we cannot die. It is my certain belief of knowledge that all the souls who have lived on this Earthly plain have left an imprint, all have to answer to the great energy we call God. If it is the will of God for me to continue my path I will do the best I can, and whatever I do I hope you will understand that LOVE cannot die. Without my family and friends I am nothing, without the people I love I do not know what I would do and the people who love me for what I am, all my faults and digressions I thank them, for I am me, the way I was made.

The World as we know it is changing, the people need to learn tolerance and forget greed for the time is coming when much is to be revealed and man needs to take stock of himself and his deeds; for we cannot continue in this earthly world as we are doing at the moment. We must respect and remember that each one of us, no matter what creed or colour, are children of one God and answerable to one God.

If I should write a fourth book - that is not up to me, all I ask is that I speak with truth, honesty and the love of God, and the help of my very special friend and Guide Abe, with whom all things are possible, if in truth.

Acknowledgements

To all the people of this world who are interested in the world to come.

Thank you for being interested in this book, I have tried to open my way of life to you and share some of my experiences.

I wish to thank my special friends and colleagues, who support me in my work, we all need friends and I hope that they understand how special friendship is.

Nancy who keeps me solvent and has always understood me and who is in fact herself a very good medium.

Brenda as always who is so often there for me. We used to travel together and shared many experiences and met many nice people; and Allan her husband for his support.

Most of all John my husband. He deserves a medal for putting up with my strange ways and my visitors of the Spirit and patience with my main topic of conversation. He has put up with me for fifty-four years, I do not know how he has and I am so grateful.

My three sons and daughters-in-law. In fact it is my chosen daughters and my very special grandchildren and great grandchildren, who keep me on my toes and hopefully young enough to enjoy their lives, especially Sarah, who has kept me sane helping with this book. When she goes to Australia shortly I will have to learn to spell, many thanks Sarah, with my love.

I never did think I would be alive to do it so I thank the other life for giving me the privilege to work for them.

Thank you to my numerous friends in Ireland, they are like second families to me.

Hannah in America whom I have great pleasure in channelling with. She and I are as one in our thoughts and our inner knowing that Spirit work very often on the same level with us both. Further information about her Retreat Centre is listed by direct e mail mountainthyme@ctechusa.com.

This retreat centre is a spiritual adventure and a unique time of reconnecting with the past, your present and the future concerns of Earth.

I have not forgotten my friend Agnes who started me on my working journey in Dalby Street, SNU, my first public demonstration in a Church many years ago.

Certainly my thanks to my Jersey friends, seen and unseen.

Jim who is a tower of strength and his unique healing energy and is such a help in fact invaluable to my work, his knowledge never ceases to amaze me, his knowledge of the Earth and all its clearing of imperfections and the clarity of his information. I am truly blessed to work with a person with such a gift; he is far above the usual perception of a healer.

Ross who worked alongside with me for a time. She made me understand how disorganised I am. Truly I am very grateful, she gave her time and expertise at a very difficult time for me. Thank you Ross.

Helen and Aine Maxi who have been there for me. I could write a book of thanks to them. I am a lucky person to have such good friends.

If you have good friends and family you can ask for nothing better.

Thank you Rhyl Church for some very happy memories.

Colwyn Bay was my first church of development and it gives me great pleasure to serve them with the outcome, of their first start for me in medium-ship training.

My priority is to thank my Guide Abe who has been always there in my work for me.

I must admit that I have found great comfort with the vibrations of music; I believe music feeds the soul with understanding especially in times of trouble and the need for peace within.

Thank you Chris, Donovan, and my friend James; each a musician in different ways. All top of their fields yet have a wonderful healing energy. They share their gifts by sound, the highest vibration connecting to medium-ship.

And of course all you patient people who read my book. I hope it helps you, if it has then I have done my job for Spirit, If not perhaps I will try again.

I hope you have enjoyed 'Walking in Two Worlds' with me and look forward to perhaps meeting you at one of my demonstrations.